KT-226-251

Contents

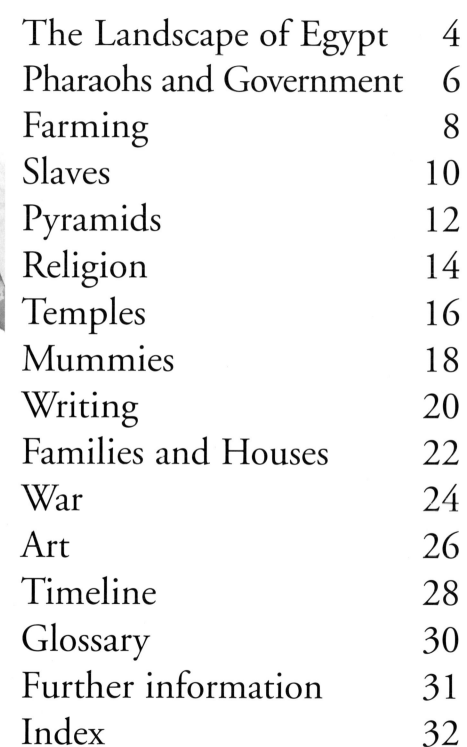

The Landscape of Egypt

Egypt is a large country in north-eastern Africa. It is a land of opposites, where sandy desert and fertile fields exist side by side. Today, Egypt is about two-thirds desert and one-third farmland and urban area. It's important to understand that the boundaries marked on today's maps show the outline of modern Egypt, which is a much larger area than the one we refer to as 'ancient Egypt'.

Ancient Egypt was a narrow strip of fertile land that lay either side of the River Nile. It was here that one of the world's greatest civilizations flourished for more than 3,000 years – and it was the River Nile that made it all possible.

LAND AND SAND
The ancient Egyptians lived and worked on a narrow strip of fertile land on either side of the River Nile. It was between 2 and 40 km wide. Beyond it lay a vast, sandy desert which they called *Deshret*, meaning 'Red Land'. Few people lived there.

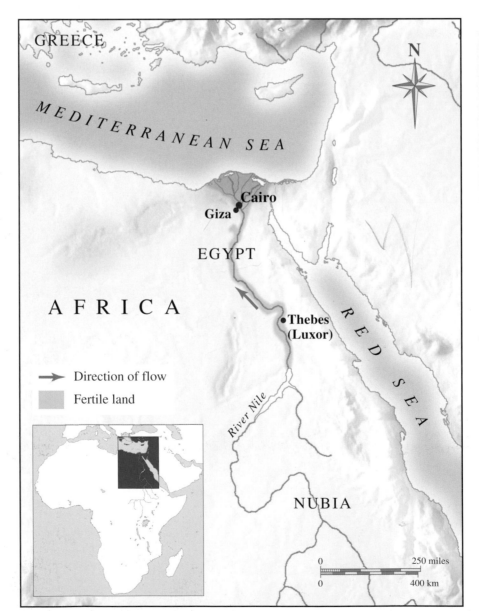

Direction of flow

Fertile land

WEBLINK
http://www.sis.gov.eg/egyptinf/culture/html/rnile.htm

Lots of information about the River Nile, from ancient times to the present day.

RIVER NILE
The River Nile flows the entire length of Egypt, from the south to the north. It is the world's longest river. From its source in Burundi, East Africa, to where it empties into the Mediterranean Sea, it is about 6,740 km long. Today, as in the past, people live along its banks, where there is good soil for farming. Beyond the fertile strip lies barren, sandy desert.

HOW DO WE KNOW?

There are many ways to learn about ancient Egypt. One is to read the words of the Egyptians themselves. Thousands of their texts have been found, and many have been translated into our own languages. Millions of real objects and thousands of structures can be examined, from pots to people (mummies), temples to tombs. We can also study the writing of early travellers, such as those of historians Herodotus (c. 485–420BCE) and Strabo (c. 64BCE–c. CE21), who described the land and its customs. Archaeologists have combined all this evidence to build a picture of life in Egypt thousands of years ago.

A Greek historian, Herodotus, visited Egypt in about 450BCE. He wrote about his visit, describing Egypt as 'the gift of the Nile'. This was a wise and accurate description. The Nile gave Egyptians water for drinking, washing and watering crops. It provided fish and water birds for food, and was used by boats to move people, animals and goods.

Most of all, the River Nile made Egypt fertile. Each summer it flooded. After the flood, a layer of black silt was left on its floodplain. This was the river's greatest gift, allowing farming to grow crops to feed the people.

Daily life depended on the Nile's annual flood, which brought new soil to old fields. It made the Egyptians believe their land was reborn every year. This was a major belief and it formed an important part of life in ancient Egypt, since people came to believe that even their own flesh-and-blood bodies could be reborn (see page 18).

Such was the importance of the Nile's black silt that the ancient Egyptians called themselves *remetch en Kemet*: 'the people of the Black Land'. The ancient Greeks called the land *Aigyptios* – from which comes our word 'Egypt'.

Pharaohs and Government

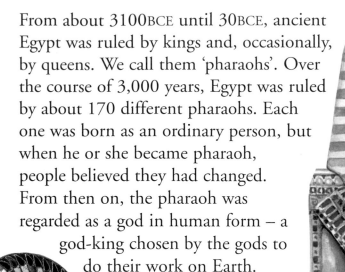

From about 3100BCE until 30BCE, ancient Egypt was ruled by kings and, occasionally, by queens. We call them 'pharaohs'. Over the course of 3,000 years, Egypt was ruled by about 170 different pharaohs. Each one was born as an ordinary person, but when he or she became pharaoh, people believed they had changed. From then on, the pharaoh was regarded as a god in human form – a god-king chosen by the gods to do their work on Earth.

The pharaoh was Egypt's supreme leader. He was head of the government, commander of the army and in charge of all the laws.

SCARAB BEETLE
The scarab beetle was a symbol of the sun-god, Khepri. Egyptians saw how the beetle rolled a ball of dung across the ground, which made them think of the invisible power that moved the sun through the sky. Also, they saw how young beetles emerged from inside the dung ball, making them think it had the power to create new life out of nothing.

ROYAL REGALIA
Pharaohs had items that symbolized their status as kings. One was the striped *nemes* headcloth. It was pulled tight across the forehead and gathered into a 'tail' at the back. Shaped flaps rested on the pharaoh's shoulders. On his forehead were vulture and cobra figures, symbols that showed the pharaoh ruled the whole of Egypt, not just a part of it.

COUNTING TAXES

The top part of this wall painting shows two kneeling scribes at work. They are writing a record of the taxes collected from farmers in a village. In the lower part of the painting the farmers' cattle are being herded together and counted.

WEBLINK

http://www.touregypt.net/
featurestories/reg.htm

Good information and images about the royal regalia of Egyptian pharaohs.

The day-to-day work of governing Egypt was done by priests, governors and overseers – thousands of them. Like our own civil servants, they worked for the government, carrying out their leader's orders. The most important official was the vizier. He was 'chief of all the king's works'. His duty was to inform the pharaoh on all matters relating to the well-being and security of Egypt, from the collection of taxes to the state of relations with Egypt's neighbours, who may, or may not, have been friendly.

The vizier was in charge of Egypt's governors, called *nomarchs*. They controlled Egypt's forty-two regional districts, or *nomes*. Each district had its own groups of officials, including scribes (record-keepers) and overseers (supervisors).

HOW DO WE KNOW?

Egypt's system of government had lots of rules and lots of people working for it. From the detailed written records made by scribes, we can see how the system worked, from top to bottom, from pharaoh to peasant. We can use the evidence of art and architecture to work out facts about the role of pharaohs and queens in society. Carved inscriptions and statues show the god-like nature and power of Egypt's rulers.

At the very bottom of society were the ordinary working people of Egypt – humble peasants who farmed the land, fished the Nile, produced the food, and built towns, temples and tombs.

Farming

Egypt was a land of farmers, but the land they farmed was not theirs. All farm land belonged to the pharaoh, not to the farmers who worked on it. Farmers were the biggest group of workers in ancient Egypt and were important for the work they did in feeding the population.

The farming year had three seasons: flood (June to October), growing (November to March) and harvesting (April to May). The flood season was when the River Nile spilled across its floodplain, leaving behind a layer of silt. After the flood, the land was divided into small, square fields which overseers shared amongst the farmers, who ploughed and planted them with the year's crops.

FARMERS' FIELD
A group of farmers prepare a field for planting. A line of men loosen the soil with wooden hoes. Behind them are men scattering seeds, followed by farm animals who walk over the field, treading the seeds into the soil – burying them out of sight of hungry birds. The seeds could then begin to grow.

PLOUGHING
Some farmers prepared the soil for planting by turning it over with wooden ploughs pulled by cattle. This is a wooden model made in ancient times of a farmer ploughing his field. It was found inside a tomb.

The main crop was wheat, which gave flour for bread and cakes. Bread was also made from barley, as was beer. Egyptian beer was a soup-like, nutritious drink. Everyone drank it – even children. Other crops were onions, leeks, garlic, peas, lentils, beans, radishes, cabbages, cucumbers and lettuces. Fruit crops included red grapes, figs, dates and pomegranates. The flax plant was grown for its fibres, which were spun to make linen for clothes.

WEBLINK
http://touregypt.net/
historicalessays/
lifeinEgypt5.htm

Lots of information and pictures about farming and hunting.

The main farm animal was the cow. It gave meat, milk and leather. Cows pulled carts and ploughs, while donkeys carried sacks of grain and trampled cereal ears to remove their grains. Sheep and goats gave meat, wool and hides. Geese, ducks and hens gave eggs and meat. Pigs were also kept for meat.

HARVESTING A WHEAT CROP

In this painting, a farmer is seen harvesting a cereal crop. He gathers a bunch of stems in one hand, then cuts the ears of grain off with a fast sweep of a sickle. His sickle is made from wood with a row of chipped flint (stone) blades fixed along its cutting edge. The blades, as sharp as broken glass, were easily replaced when they became blunt.

After the harvest, overseers counted the sacks of grain a farmer had produced, and scribes made a record. The farmer was given some of the grain as payment for his work, and some was taken from him, which was a tax he had to pay to the pharaoh.

HOW DO WE KNOW?

Ancient Egyptian paintings and models show images of farmers at work. This is excellent evidence that helps us learn facts that would otherwise be hard to discover. The model above shows how a farmer held his plough, and what it looked like. The tomb painting **above** shows that a farmer cut the ears of wheat or barley from his plants, leaving their stems standing. They were cut later for straw. Egyptian objects have survived, such as flint blades from sickles and millstones from grinding cereals. Archaeologists have also found animal and plant remains, including bones, grains, pollen and food – all preserved by Egypt's dry climate.

Slaves

PRISONERS OF WAR

Prisoners of war from Nubia, to the south of Egypt, were forced into slavery and became the lowest members of Egyptian society. Some went on to join the Egyptian army and fight in the pharaoh's wars.

Throughout history slaves have been used as 'useful tools', owned by, and working for the benefit of, other people. However, unlike in ancient Greece or Rome, where slavery was a common and accepted practice, Egyptian society functioned perfectly well without the need for masses of slaves. There was some slavery in Egypt, but it never seems to have been of great importance.

Slaves began to appear in Egyptian society only after Egypt's pharaohs began fighting wars with their neighbours, from around 2000BCE onwards. Soldiers were captured and it was these prisoners-of-war who became slaves in Egypt. Prisoners came areas north-east of Egypt, Nubia (present-day Sudan, south of Egypt), and from a land in east Africa which the Egyptians called Punt, thought to be Eritrea (Ethiopia) or Somalia.

HOW DO WE KNOW?

Slavery leaves few traces. There are no obvious differences between a slave's skeleton and a free person's. Both may show signs of a life of hard work – but it is impossible to say if the person was (or was not) a slave. Evidence for slavery comes from Egyptian writings. They talk about slaves being taken in battle, slaves working for people, and slaves sold, given away or freed. Pharaoh Thutmose III said he made 90,000 prisoners into slaves. Ramesses III said he gave 113,000 to temples. Both figures are probably exaggerated.

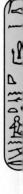

JAR CARRIER
This statue may be a Nubian man or, because the jar he is holding appears so large, perhaps he is a pygmy (pygmies were brought to Egypt to work in temples).

Prisoners of war who became slaves in Egypt were put to work on a range of tasks. Some worked as labourers on building projects and in the gold and copper mines of Nubia, and others were found work on farms and in temples. Some became servants for the royal family and nobles, working in their palaces and homes as domestic helpers.

It wasn't only foreigners who became slaves – some Egyptians themselves entered a life of slavery. These were people who had fallen into debt, or were too poor to feed and house themselves. They must have been desperate, since they volunteered to become slaves. They knew that their owners would at least provide

WEBLINK
http://nefertiti.iwebland. com/timelines/topics/ slavery.htm

A look at slaves and the concept of slavery in Egyptian society.

HOUSEHOLD SERVANTS
Some slaves worked as household servants. For them, life was comfortable and they were treated well by their owners. Slaves were often set free. Owners did this because they hoped one day they would be reborn in the next life – and this could only happen if they had done good things in this life.

Pyramids

PYRAMID BUILDING

Pyramids were built by an efficient and highly organized workforce. Stone blocks were brought from nearby quarries, then dragged up ramps of soil to their positions on the pyramid.

After a pharaoh died, his (or her) body was buried inside a specially built tomb. Egypt's first pharaohs were laid to rest in massive tombs built from blocks of stone. They had square bases and four sloping triangular sides which met at a point. We call these tombs 'pyramids'.

Most pyramids were built during the time archaeologists call the Old Kingdom. This was the 'golden age' of pyramid building. The first pyramid went up in about 2600BCE, and about ninety were built during the following 800 years.

A STONE-WORKER'S TOOLS

Stone was cut and shaped using simple tools. Blocks were cut from the rockface with hammer-stones, copper chisels and wooden wedges. Tools, like the ones on the right, were used at the building site to smooth the surfaces of the blocks. These tools were probably also used to carve statues.

The Egyptians built pyramids because they believed they connected Earth to heaven. The first pyramid ever built, for the pharaoh Djoser, was a series of six platforms, one on top of the other. It's called the Step Pyramid, because of its step-like appearance. Perhaps pyramids were thought of as 'stairways', up which a pharaoh would ascend as he travelled to heaven.

Egypt's best-known pyramids are at Giza, on the outskirts of Cairo, the present-day capital city. Three large pyramids were built there, for the pharaohs Khufu, Khafre and Menkaure (father, son and grandson). Unlike Djoser's Step Pyramid, the Giza pyramids were not built in a series of rising steps. Instead, they were made with smooth sides. They are 'true' pyramids.

Pyramids were supposed to be safe places in which to bury Egypt's pharaohs. However, every one of them was broken into by tomb raiders in ancient times. They stole the precious contents meant for the pharaohs to use in the next life (see page 18), and showed no respect for the kings' bodies, ripping into them in search of valuable items to steal.

WEBLINK

http://www.pbs.org/wgbh/nova/pyramid/explore/

Find out about the Giza pyramids, who built them, and how.

HOW DO WE KNOW?

Our understanding of pyramids – what they were, who built them, and how – comes from many sources. There are the pyramids themselves, which have been examined inside and out. The quarries their stones came from have been found, and the villages where the workers lived have been excavated, as have their graves. Their skeletons reveal the injuries workers suffered, from broken and crushed bones to curved spines from moving heavy loads. Experiments have been carried out with copies of tools used by the workers. They reveal the likely methods used to cut and move the stone.

GIZA PYRAMIDS

Two of the three pyramids at Giza. On the left is the pyramid of Khafre, still with part of its smooth outer casing near the top. On the right is the pyramid of Khufu, known as the Great Pyramid. Built from an estimated 2.3 million blocks of stone, the Great Pyramid was 146.6 metres tall. It took about twenty-three years to build this gigantic structure.

Pyramids took a long time to build, needed massive amounts of stone and a large workforce – and they were easy to break into. For these reasons, pyramids went out of fashion. They were replaced by tombs cut into the sides of a rocky valley, where it was hoped the kings of Egypt would find perfect peace for ever.

Religion

The ancient Egyptians believed that a supreme power controlled the Universe and everything in it. However, they didn't believe in one all-powerful controlling god or goddess. Instead, they believed in many deities – perhaps as many as 2,000 different ones. (No one knows the actual number of gods and goddesses worshipped in ancient Egypt).

Most were 'local gods'. These deities were minor beings worshipped in just a few towns and villages, and who were unknown elsewhere in the land. Some were 'personal gods', worshipped by a family or a group of people. For example, they might decide that a cat, which always came looking for food, was a god in disguise. They'd care for it, feed it and offer prayers to it. In return for these gifts, they hoped their very own personal god would protect them. (To anyone else though, it was just a cat scrounging a meal.)

Among the many gods and goddesses were ones that everyone worshipped. These were the most important and powerful deities of them all. Some are shown on these pages.

WEBLINK
http://www.ancientegypt.
co.uk/gods/home.html

Information and images from the British Museum about ancient Egypt's religion, gods and myths.

OSIRIS
The skin of Osiris was coloured green – the colour of new life (the colour of the plants in farmers' fields). Green represented being born again. People called Osiris the 'eternally good being'.

GODS AND GODDESSES
Isis: goddess of fertility and nature.
Ra: god of creation; father of the gods.
Osiris: god of the afterlife, the dead, and judge of the dead.
Seth: god of chaos, storms and evil.
Thoth: god of wisdom, writing, reading, mathematics and magic.

Isis   Ra   Osiris   Seth   Thoth

Aten

Anubis

Horus

Bastet

Amun-Ra

GODS AND GODDESSES

Amun-Ra: god of creation and king of the gods.
Aten: god of daylight and warmth, bringer of life to the world.
Bastet: goddess of joy, the home and the warmth of the sun.
Anubis: god of embalming and the keeper of secrets.
Horus: god of the sky, the rising sun, eternal life, and keeper of order.

Temples were built in honour of these great gods – homes in which their spirits were said to live (see page 16). Because people believed they had to please the gods, they offered them prayers and gifts. They believed that, in return, the gods protected the people and looked after Egypt. Without this divine protection it was thought the world would sink into total chaos – and the powers of evil would take over.

Religious festivals were held throughout the year. On these great occasions a god's sacred statue was taken from its temple and carried in a procession. Because the god's spirit was thought to dwell within the statue, people worshipped it as it passed by them – they thought they were in the presence of the god.

HOW DO WE KNOW?

The ancient Egyptians have left us many clues about their religion. Temples show us the homes they built for their gods, and statues and paintings reveal how people thought the gods looked. We can read prayers offered to the gods, and stories (myths) tell us how the gods were related to each other, and what deeds they did. The gods were responsible for everything, from the creation of the sky and the Earth to the flooding of the River Nile, which happened, so it was said, when the goddess Isis cried and her tears splashed into it.

AMUN-RA

Amun-Ra was shown as a man wearing a crown topped with feathered plumes. He became the main god during the New Kingdom (from about 1500BCE). His name means 'Invisible One'.

Temples

PRIESTS

Priests shaved off all their body hair, including their eyebrows. They did this to purify themselves, cleansing their bodies of anything that might offend the temple's god.

There were two types of temple in ancient Egypt. One was built to honour a dead pharaoh and is known as a royal or mortuary temple. The other type was built in honour of a god or goddess.

The ancient Egyptian word for a god's temple is *hat-netcher*, which means 'god's house'. It was called this because people believed the spirit of a deity actually lived inside it. Temples were the most important buildings in a town. Some towns, such as Thebes, the capital of ancient Egypt, had several temples next to each other, forming complexes where hundreds of people worked.

Temples were more than centres of religion. They had workshops where objects for temple use were made, grain stores, schools for scribes and priests, and libraries of book-scrolls. Because they owned land and mines, temples were wealthy places.

TEMPLE OF AMUN, LUXOR

A temple, such as this one at Luxor, on the east bank of the River Nile, was a god's home on Earth. This temple was built for the god Amun. (Inside it is a Muslim mosque, built in the CE1200s.)

SACRED STATUE

The god's spirit was believed to live inside a sacred statue kept inside the temple's holiest room. In the morning, and at night, priests washed the statue to show respect for the deity. They anointed it with oil, dressed it in clean clothes, burned sweet-smelling incense to drive away evil, and brought food to feed the god. Only the most senior priests could enter this innermost sanctuary, where they felt they were in the presence of the god they served.

Unlike today's religious buildings (churches, mosques, synagogues), where worshippers come and go as they please, the public were only allowed into certain parts of Egyptian temples, such as the open courtyard areas. The rest of the temple was only open to priests.

Priests called themselves 'servants of the gods', or even 'slaves of the gods'. They lived in the temples where they worked, serving the gods by offering them gifts and prayers, and by leading ceremonies. All this work was designed to please the gods. People believed that if the gods were respected and made to feel happy, then they would continue to live in their temple homes on Earth and protect Egypt.

Temples were built to last, and we can walk where priests and worshippers once did. The massive Temple of Karnak, Thebes, is the most awesome of them all. Known to the ancient Egyptians as *Ipet-isut* ('The Most Select of Places'), it covers 100 hectares, and one room is a forest of 134 giant stone columns. An Egyptian text says that the god Amun told the pharaoh Hatshepsut to build a temple: 'May you build a house, may you embellish a sanctuary, may you consecrate my godly place.'

WEBLINK

http://www.eyelid.co.uk/karnak1.htm

All about the Temple of Karnak, Thebes, the largest of all temples in ancient Egypt, built for the god Amun.

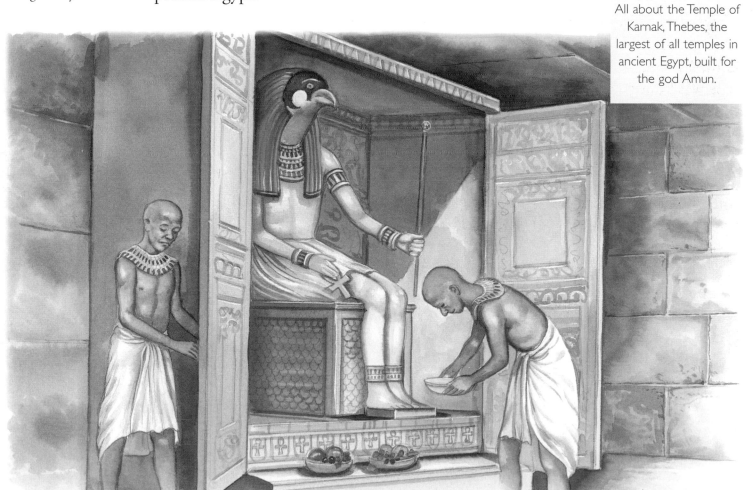

Mummies

One of the biggest mysteries is what, if anything, happens after death. The ancient Egyptians thought they knew. They believed that after a person died they began a long and difficult journey which led them to the next world (the afterlife), where they were reborn and lived forever. They were not afraid to die, because they thought of death as the next stage in a person's life cycle. Egyptians said death was the 'night of going forth to life'. But a person could only be reborn in their new life if their body was saved from decay – and this is why the Egyptians preserved their dead. It took seventy days to make a mummy. Embalmers worked on the west bank of the River Nile. This was the side of the river linked with death and the afterlife, because the sun set (died) in the west before rising (being reborn) to live again.

A family handed the body of a dead person to the embalmers. After cleansing, it was laid on a sloping table. The brain, thought to be unimportant, was removed from the skull through the left nostril. It was thrown away. The intestines, stomach, lungs and liver were taken out through a cut in the left side of the abdomen. The heart (the Egyptians thought it controlled the body) and the kidneys were left inside. All this took fifteen days.

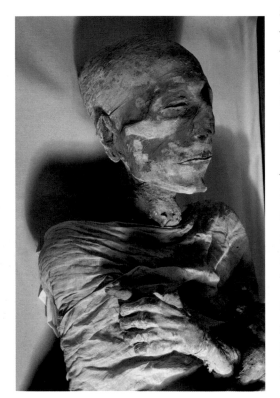

WEBLINK
http://www.national geographic.com/media/ tv/mummy/index.html

You'll find more information on how to make a mummy here.

HOW DO WE KNOW?

No 'instruction manuals' have survived from ancient Egypt that tell us how or why the Egyptians made mummies. Perhaps they never wrote any. But what we do have are accounts written by ancient Greeks. Herodotus (writing in the 450sBCE) gives a long description. (It is from him that we know it took seventy days to make a mummy.). Diodorus Siculus (writing in the 50sBCE) comments on the embalmer, known as the 'slitter', who cut the abdomen open and was then chased away for violating a corpse. And, of course, there are the mummies themselves. They've been examined in great detail, from bone X-rays to the DNA analysis of their genes.

For the next forty days the body lay under a heap of natron –
a salty white powder from the shores of a lake. It dried the
body by drawing moisture from it. Then, the body cavity was
packed (often with old rags) so it looked lifelike again, and
the skin was rubbed with oils and coated with resin.

In the final fifteen days the mummified body was wrapped
from head to toe in linen strips, placed in a coffin and handed
back to its family for burial.

NEST OF COFFINS
A wrapped mummy was
placed in a wooden
coffin which was usually
decorated, like the one
seen here made for a
noble person.
Some mummies were
protected by a 'nest' of
coffins, where one fitted
inside another.

CANOPIC JARS
Embalmers usually put a
person's mummified
organs into jars. Known
as 'canopic jars', each
was decorated with an
image of the god who
protected the organ
it held. These jars were
intestines, falcon-headed
Qebehsenuef (above left)
and lungs, baboon-
headed Hapi (above
right). Others (not
shown above) were
stomach (jackal-headed
Duamutef); liver
(human-headed
Imseti).

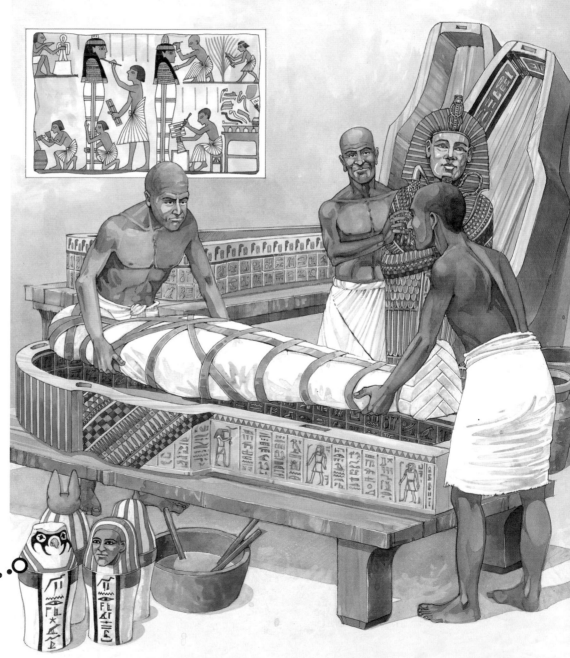

Writing

SCRIBE AT WORK
A scribe usually worked sitting cross-legged on the ground. He stretched his kilt (like a skirt) tight against his knees, and this made a flat surface for him to rest on. He used his left hand to hold and unroll the papyrus paper. In his right hand he held a reed brush or pen. He wrote in red or black ink.

Writing is a key feature of all advanced civilizations. The ancient Egyptians discovered writing in about 3100BCE, and from then on they wrote about their world in great detail.

They believed that writing, like many other aspects of society, was invented by the gods and given to humankind as a gift. This is why the Egyptians called writing *medu-netjer* ('words of the gods'), and why they believed it was sacred.

Even through writing was so important, very few people – perhaps only one in ten – could read or write. However, there was one group of workers (always men) who were highly literate. These were scribes. They read and wrote letters for people, kept records of goods owned by temples and the pharaoh, and made copies of texts about religion, science and medicine.

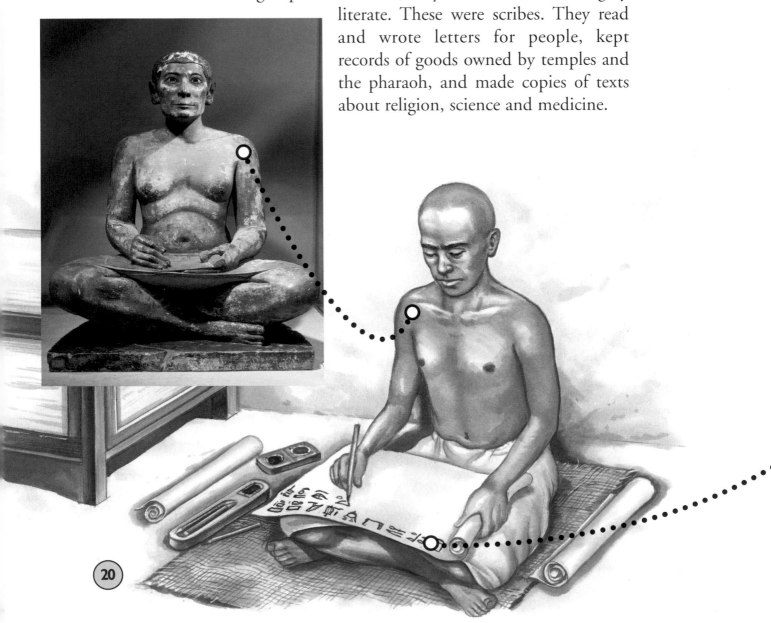

WEBLINK

http://touregypt.net/
ename/

A fun page where you can convert your name into Egyptian hieroglyphs.

The Egyptian language could be written in three different scripts. For everyday writing, scribes used a script that was quick to write. It's called hieratic (Greek for 'priestly'), but in about 600BCE it was replaced by demotic (Greek for 'popular'), which was an easier and faster script to write. There were also signs for numbers: units, tens, hundreds and thousands.

The third script was slow to write, and was mainly used for sacred texts. It's called hieroglyphics (Greek for 'holy signs'), and it's Egypt's most famous script. Scribes learned some 750 picture signs, which they wrote left to right, right to left, or in columns. Hieroglyphic texts were written on papyrus, painted on the walls of tombs, and carved in stone.

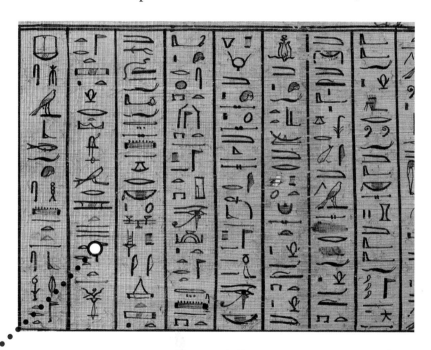

HIEROGLYPHICS

The hieroglyphic script was used for 3,500 years, from about 3100BCE to about CE400. This example is written in black ink (made from soot or charcoal) on papyrus paper. This type of paper was made from the papyrus water reed, which grew on the banks of the River Nile. A scribe wrote with brushes and pens. It took time for the ink to dry, so the scribe had to be careful not to smudge his work.

HOW DO WE KNOW?

Paintings and models of scribes show them at work, and many examples of their pens, brushes and writing cases have been found. A scribe named Khety wrote about his job: 'It's the most important of all occupations. If you can write, you will be better off than everyone else.' His statement tells us about the status of scribes in Egyptian society. There are thousands of examples of Egyptian writing, both in Egypt and in collections around the world. Hieroglyphs were first deciphered in 1822, by a Frenchman called Jean-François Champollion. Now, many experts can read the words of the ancient Egyptians themselves.

Families and Houses

A 'typical' family in ancient Egypt was a husband and wife and their children. The average number of children in a family was five. (These were the ones who lived, but others probably died when they were babies.)

Before they could start a family, a man and a woman had to get married to each other. Marriage in ancient Egypt was not based on any religious or civil customs, unlike marriages today. There was no special ceremony, no special place to get married in, and no special officials to marry the couple. Instead, a marriage was a legal agreement made between two families. They agreed how much property the man and the woman were to bring into the marriage, all of which was described in a written list. The property list formed the marriage contract. To keep property within a family, it was common for relatives (usually cousins) to marry each other.

HOUSES

Houses were made from sun-dried mud-brick. They were small and often joined together in groups that shared walls. Inside were one or two living rooms, and a kitchen with a hearth. They were single-storey buildings with flat roofs. Most people had few, if any, pieces of furniture, since wood was scarce and expensive.

WEBLINK
http://www2.sptimes.com/Egypt/EgyptCredit.4.2.html

Information about family life, marriage, children, housing, and more.

22

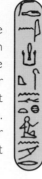

Paintings and models show images of couples and *all* the children they have had. (Even children who had died are included, to suggest they would rejoin their family in the afterlife.) Texts known as 'wisdom literature' give advice and instructions for what is acceptable (and what is not) in family life. For example, the text known as the *Wisdom of Ptah-hotep* (a vizier) advises that a man should: 'Love your wife dearly. Feed her well, clothe her in style. Keep her happy as long as you live. Thus will you make her stay in your house.' A happy home in ancient Egypt was just as important then as it is today.

Women married when they were 12 or 13 years old; men when they were 14 or 15. We would say they were still children, but to the Egyptians they were adults. The reason for marrying young was simple: people's lives were short. Studies on the mummies of noble people, who lived privileged lives, show that men and women died, on average, in their mid-thirties. Humble, hard-working peasants died in their twenties. Early marriages were, therefore, essential in order to produce the next generation of farmers, scribes, brick-makers, tomb-builders, officials, priests, embalmers, and so on.

As well as bearing lots of children, a woman's duty was to look after the family home – she was 'Mistress of the House'. A man's duty was to provide for his family.

BOARD GAME

The most popular game played in ancient Egypt was *senet* – the game of 'passing'. It was played on boards, like the one seen here, or on grids scratched on to flat stones. A game for two players, each player had seven pieces. The aim of the game was to move the pieces around the board's thirty squares, which represented good and bad omens. The first player to move all his or her pieces to the end was the winner.

FAMILY GROUP

A limestone model of a husband, wife and their son and daughter, made about 1500BCE. Their arms are around each other's shoulders, which is a sign of their family bond. They are all wearing wigs. The mother has a false beard, a symbol used in art to show that a person had died, and had been reborn in the afterlife. This model probably comes from her tomb.

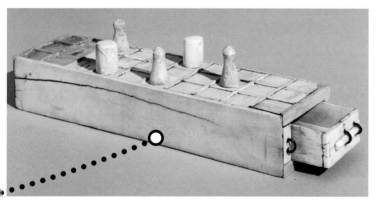

War

STRONG BOW

The archer's bow was a powerful weapon. The best ones were made from different materials glued together in three layers. Known as composite bows, they had an outer layer of horn, a wooden central core and an inner layer of sinew. This type of bow could shoot an arrow 175 metres – two to three times further than an arrow shot from an ordinary wooden bow.

Ancient Egypt's first soldiers were conscripts: men forced to fight in the pharaoh's army. They were part-time soldiers who were sent home to their everyday jobs after their army duty ended. This system lasted for about 1,500 years, but at the start of the New Kingdom, about 1500 BCE, it changed. From then on, the pharaoh's army was made up of soldiers who worked full time – not just in wartime, but also in times of peace.

However, the conscript system didn't completely disappear. If a New Kingdom pharaoh needed to quickly increase the size of his army, perhaps because of a war, he took men from the civilian population – usually about one man in every ten.

Foot soldiers were organized into large units (divisions) of about 5,000 men. A division was made up of smaller units of about 250 men (companies) and fifty men (platoons). In total, the New Kingdom army had about 20,000 soldiers, usually led by a son of the pharaoh.

24

The army also had chariots. They were lightweight, two-wheeled vehicles pulled by pairs of horses. Two men rode inside a chariot – a charioteer who steered it and a soldier (usually an archer or spear-thrower). A chariot's top speed was around 40 kph. In battle, chariots were moving platforms for archers and spear-throwers. They were driven up to the enemy so they could use their weapons at close range. Chariots attacked from many directions. They charged through front lines of soldiers to cause panic, or came at them from the sides, or even from behind.

WEBLINK
http://www.touregypt.net/featurestories/war.htm

Lots of information and pictures about the ancient Egyptian army, with links to weapons, chariots and battles.

IMAGES OF WAR
Images of Egyptian soldiers, chariots, battle scenes and prisoners of war, were carved in stone for all to see. They were designed to make ordinary people feel proud of their army and its victories.

HOW DO WE KNOW?

We know about the Egyptian army from evidence left behind by the Egyptians. For example, carvings on temple walls tell us about a great battle fought in about 1275BCE at the city of Kadesh in present-day Syria. This is an example of historical evidence, from the point of view of the Egyptians. In the battle, the pharaoh Ramesses II led 20,000 soldiers against the Hittites (a warlike people whose homeland was in modern-day Turkey). In truth, the battle was a draw – but Ramesses decided he had won it, which is how it is shown in the carvings. Archaeologists have also found real objects, from arrowheads to chariots. They show how troops were equipped, and how good their weapons were.

WEAPONS AND ARMOUR
Foot soldiers fought with spears, axes, curved swords and daggers. They did not wear armour, but protected themselves with leather or wooden shields, like the one above.

Art

The ancient Egyptians created works of art from a wide range of natural materials. Sculptors shaped stone, such as hard basalt and soft limestone, into statues and relief carvings (flat panels on which images stand out from the background). Jewellers used semi-precious stones such as green feldspar, orange-red carnelian, mauve amethyst, red jasper and dark blue lapis lazuli to make beads and amulets (protective charms). Egypt's jewellers also worked with metals, especially silver and gold, making finger-rings, pendants, brooches and mummy masks. Because gold never lost its shine, it was regarded as a divine, holy substance – the flesh of the gods. Other metals, such as copper and bronze, were made into small statues. Carpenters used wood for models of people at work (such as the one on page 9), and for furniture.

WEBLINK

http://www.metmuseum.org/explore/newegypt/htm/th_frame.htm

Excellent information about Egyptian art from the Metropolitan Museum of Art, New York, featuring objects from the Museum collection.

BODY IMAGE

The human body was painted as if it could be seen from many angles. Head, face and limbs were shown from the side; eyes, shoulders and chest from the front; hips, legs and feet from the side.

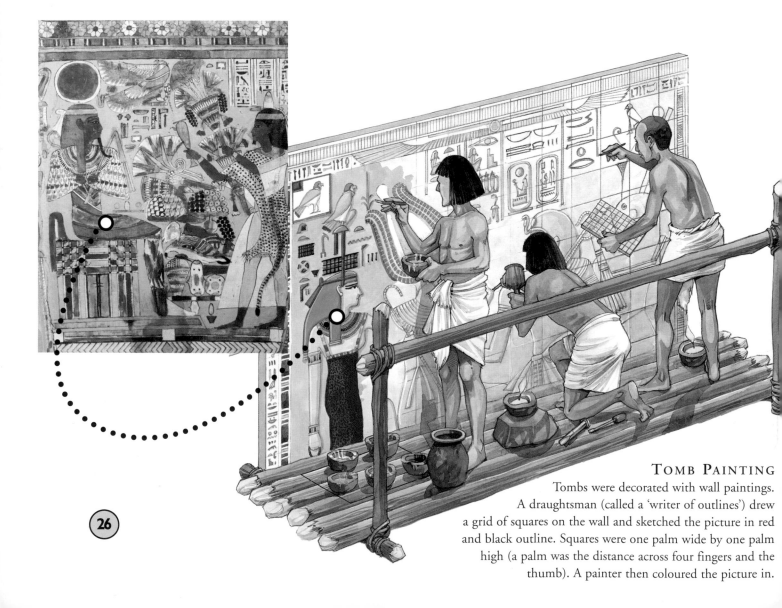

TOMB PAINTING

Tombs were decorated with wall paintings. A draughtsman (called a 'writer of outlines') drew a grid of squares on the wall and sketched the picture in red and black outline. Squares were one palm wide by one palm high (a palm was the distance across four fingers and the thumb). A painter then coloured the picture in.

Most raw materials were found in Egypt, but lapis lazuli was not. The Egyptians, who called this blue stone *khesbed*, got it from merchants who brought it from Afghanistan, some 3,200 km east of Egypt. Lapis lazuli was so highly prized, the Egyptians produced a 'copy-cat' substance that looked like it. We call it faience. Made from a paste of crushed quartz, coated with blue or green glaze, it was shaped into figures, amulets and jewellery, then baked hard in an oven.

In Egyptian art, such as tomb paintings, colours had meanings. White was for joy; yellow for gold and the gods; pale yellow for women's skin, brownish-red for men's skin; red for blood and life, and also for evil and chaos; green for water and new life; blue for sky; and black for soil and fertility.

HOW DO WE KNOW?

Art objects are found in tombs and temples, workshops and villages, and are studied to find out what they are made from, and how they were made. Images of craftworkers at work show the tools they used, and texts tell us about the people themselves. In a text known as the *Satire of the Trades*, a carpenter (whose tool is an adze) is compared with a farmer (who uses a hoe). It says: 'The carpenter who wields an adze, he is wearier than any field labourer. His field is the timber and his hoe is the adze. His labour is never-ending.'

QUEEN'S HEAD
This remarkable painted limestone bust (right) is one of the most famous Egyptian works of art. It is a portrait of Queen Nefertiti (c.1380-1340BCE), wife of Pharaoh Akhenaten. It is remarkable because the sculptor, a man named Thutmose, created a true likeness of the queen (most Egyptian portraits are not true to life, but show stylized images). The bust was not finished (one eye is unpainted), and it may have been used by the sculptor for teaching trainee artists.

Timeline

A NOTE ABOUT DATES
Ancient Egyptian history is divided into three large parts, known as the Old, Middle and New Kingdoms. Smaller parts are known as periods. The pharaohs are ordered into 31 dynasties, or groups. This simplified table lists the dynasties, their approximate dates and the dates that some pharaohs reigned.

All dates are BCE ('before the Common Era'). BCE dates are counted back from the year 1, which is taken to be the beginning of the Common Era. There was no year 0. These dates work in the same way as BC (before Christ) and AD (*Anno Domini*, 'the year of Our Lord'). Some dates have a 'c' in front of them. This stands for '*circa*', which means 'about'. These dates are guesses, because no one knows what the real date is.

PRE-DYNASTIC PERIOD
c. 5500-3100BCE
- Before Egypt was ruled by pharaohs.

EARLY DYNASTIC PERIOD
c. 3100-2686BCE
- First pharaohs.
- Egypt united as one land.
- First hieroglyphs written.

1st Dynasty 3100-2890BCE
  Narmer (first pharaoh, 3100BCE)
2nd Dynasty 2890-2686BCE

OLD KINGDOM
c. 2686-2181BCE
- Powerful pharaohs.
- First pyramids built.

3rd Dynasty 2686-2613BCE
  Sanakht (2686-2667BCE)
  Djoser (2667-2648BCE)
  Sekhemkhet (2648-2640BCE)
  Khaba (2640-2637BCE)
  Huni (2637-2613BCE)
4th Dynasty 2613-2494BCE
  Sneferu (2613-2589BCE)
  Khufu (2589-2566BCE)
  Djedefre (2566-2558BCE)
  Khufu (2589-2566BCE)
  Khafre (2558-2532BCE)
  Menkaure (2532-2503BCE)
  Shepseskaf (2503-2498BCE)
5th Dynasty 2494-2345BCE
  Userkaf (2494-2487BCE)
  Sahure (2487-2475BCE)
  Neferirkare (2475-2455BCE)
  Shepseskare (2455-2448BCE)
  Raneferef (2448-2445BCE)
  Nyuserre (2445-2421BCE)
  Menkauhor (2421-2414BCE)
  Djedkare (2414-2375BCE)
  Unas (2375-2345BCE)
6th Dynasty 2345-2181BCE
  Teti (2345-2323BCE)
  Userkere (2323-2321BCE)
  Pepi I (2321-2287BCE)
  Merenre (2287-2278BCE)
  Pepi II (2278-2184BCE)
  Nitiqret (2184-2181BCE)

FIRST INTERMEDIATE PERIOD
c. 2181-2055BCE
- Many minor pharaohs.

7th-8th Dynasties 2181-2125BCE
9th-10th Dynasties 2160-2025BCE
11th Dynasty 2125-2055BCE

MIDDLE KINGDOM
c. 2055-1650BCE
• Powerful pharaohs return.
11th Dynasty 2055-1985BCE
Mentuhotep II (2055-2004BCE)
Mentuhotep III (2004-1992BCE)
Mentuhotep IV (1992-1985BCE)
12th Dynasty 1985-1795BCE
Amenemhet I (1985-1955BCE)
Senusret I (1965-1920BCE)
Amenemhet II (1922-1878BCE)
Senusret II (1880-1874BCE)
Senusret III (1874-1855BCE)
Amenemhet III (1855-1808BCE)
Amenemhet IV (1808-1799BCE)
Queen Sobeknerfu (1799-1795BCE)
13th-14th Dynasties 1795-1650BCE
About 70 minor pharaohs

SECOND INTERMEDIATE PERIOD
c. 1650-1550BCE
• Egypt ruled by foreign kings.
15th-16th Dynasties 1650-1550BCE
17th Dynasty 1650-1550BCE

NEW KINGDOM
c. 1550-1069BCE
• Egypt at its most powerful.
• Pharaohs buried in rock-cut tombs.
• Expeditions to foreign lands.
• Changes made to religion.
18th Dynasty 1550-1295BCE
Ahmose I (1550-1525BCE)
Amenhotep I (1525-1504BCE)
Tuthmosis I (1504-1492BCE)
Tuthmosis II (1492-1479BCE)
Tuthmosis III (1479-1425BCE)
Queen Hatshepsut (1473-1458BCE)
Amenhotep II (1427-1400BCE)
Tuthmosis IV (1400-1390BCE)
Amenhotep III (1390-1352BCE)
Amenhotep IV (Akhenaten) (1352-1336BCE)
Smenkhkare (1338-1336BCE)
Tutankhamun (1336-1327BCE)
Ay (1327-1323BCE)
Horemheb (1323-1295BCE)
19th Dynasty 1295-1186BCE
Ramesses I (1295-1294BCE)
Seti I (1294-1279BCE)
Ramesses II (1279-1213BCE)
Merneptah (1213-1203BCE)
Amenmessu (1203-1200BCE)
Seti II (1200-1194BCE)
Siptah (1194-1188BCE)
Queen Tausret (1188-1186BCE)
20th Dynasty 1186-1069BCE
Sethnakhte (1186-1184BCE)
Ramesses III (1184-1153BCE)
Ramesses IV (1153-1147BCE)
Ramesses V (1147-1143BCE)
Ramesses VI (1143-1136BCE)
Ramesses VII (1136-1129BCE)
Ramesses VIII (1129-1126BCE)
Ramesses IX (1126-1108BCE)
Ramesses X (1108-1099BCE)
Ramesses XI (1099-1069BCE)

THIRD INTERMEDIATE PERIOD
c. 1069-715BCE
• Unsettled time.
• Rule by joint pharaohs.
21st Dynasty 1069-945BCE
22nd Dynasty 945-715BCE
23rd Dynasty 818-715BCE
24th Dynasty 727-715BCE

LATE DYNASTIC PERIOD
c. 747-332BCE
• A further unsettled time.
• Rule by joint pharaohs.
• Pharaohs from foreign lands.
25th Dynasty 747-656BCE
26th Dynasty 664-525BCE
27th Dynasty 525-404BCE
28th Dynasty 404-399BCE
29th Dynasty 399-380BCE
30th Dynasty 380-343BCE
31st Dynasty 343-332BCE

THE GRAECO-ROMAN PERIOD
332-30BCE
• Egypt belongs to the Greek empire of Alexander the Great.
• Egypt then becomes a province of the Roman Empire.
• Egypt's last two pharaohs are:
Queen Cleopatra VII (51-30BCE)
Ptolemy XV Caesarion (44-30BCE)

Glossary

Archaeologist A person who finds out about the past by looking for the remains of buildings and other objects, often beneath the ground.

Amulet A good luck charm used to protect the wearer from harm.

BCE Used in dates. Means 'before the Common Era'.

Bronze A hard metal made by mixing copper with tin.

CE Used in dates. Means 'the Common Era'. The Common Era begins with year 1, which is the same as the year AD1 in the Christian calendar.

Cereal A grass, such as wheat or barley, that produces a grain used for food.

Conscript Someone who has been forced to join an army.

Deity A god or goddess; a supreme being.

Dynasty A series of pharaohs from related families. Egypt's pharaohs formed 31 dynasties.

Embalmer A person who preserves a dead body to prevent it from decaying.

Faience A blue or green glossy material made from a baked paste of crushed quartz.

Floodplain An area of low-lying ground next to a river that often gets flooded.

Hieroglyphics The oldest writing script used in ancient Egypt, consisting of signs that refer to the meaning and sound of words.

Historian An expert in, or a student of, history.

Lapis lazuli A highly-prized dark blue stone used for amulets and jewellery.

Mortuary A room or building in which dead bodies are kept until they are buried.

Mud-brick A building brick made from clay, often mixed with chopped straw or grass, and dried hard by the sun.

Mummy An animal or human body preserved by drying.

Papyrus A water reed used to make a type of writing paper, baskets, ropes, sandals and medicine. Its root could be eaten, and burned as fuel.

Pharaoh A king or queen of ancient Egypt.

Pomegranate A round fruit with a golden skin, containing many segments of red flesh.

Pyramids Tombs with a square base and four sloping sides, built to hold the mummified body of a pharaoh.

Relief A picture cut into stone, so that figures stand out.

Sanctuary A sacred place.

Scribe A person who writes or keeps records.

Silt A type of fine sediment carried in water which settles to form mud and soil.

Slave A person who is owned completely by another, often a prisoner of war.

Tax Money paid to the government.

Temple A holy building which the Egyptians believed was the home of a god, where priests carried out religious ceremonies.

Texts Pieces of writing.

Tomb A monument containing the body of a dead person.

Further information

BOOKS

ANCIENT EGYPT
Ancient Egypt (Eyewitness Guides) by George Hart (Dorling Kindersley, 1990)
Cultural Atlas for Young People: Ancient Egypt by Geraldine Harris (Facts on File, 1990)
Everyday Life in Ancient Egypt by Neil Morris (British Museum Press, 2003)
Mummies and the Secrets of Ancient Egypt (MegaBites Series) by John Malam (Dorling Kindersley, 2001)
A Visitor's Guide to Ancient Egypt by Lesley Simms (Usborne, 2000)

HIEROGLYPHICS
Egyptian Hieroglyphs by Richard Parkinson (British Museum Press, 2003)

HOME AND FAMILY LIFE
Ancient Egypt: Family Life by Stewart Ross (Hodder Wayland, 2003)
Ancient Egypt: Food and Feasts by Stewart Ross (Hodder Wayland, 2001)
Ancient Egyptian Homes by Brenda Williams (Heinemann, 2002)

MUMMIES
Kingfisher Knowledge: Mummies by John Malam (Kingfisher, 2003)
Mummy (Eyewitness Guides) by James Putnam (Dorling Kindersley, 1993)
My Best Book of Mummies by Philip Steele (Kingfisher, 1998)
See Through History: Mummies by John Malam (Running Press, 2003)

PHARAOHS
Ancient Egypt: Pharaohs by Stewart Ross (Hodder Wayland, 2001)
Tutankhamun: the Life and Death of a Pharaoh by David Murdoch (Dorling Kindersley, 1998)

RELIGION, TEMPLES, GODS AND GODDESSES
Ancient Egyptian Gods and Goddesses by George Hart (British Museum Press, 2001)
Gods and Goddesses of Ancient Egypt by Leon Ashworth (Cherrytree Press, 2001)
Gods and Goddesses in the Daily Life of the Ancient Egyptians by Henrietta McCall (Hodder Wayland, 2003)

WORK
Ancient Egyptian Jobs by John Malam (Heinemann. 2002)

CD-ROMS
Ancient Egypt – Heinemann Explore History KS2 (Heinemann)
Ancient Egyptians (Anglia Multimedia Ltd, 1997)
Egyptians (Interface Series, Two-Can Publishing, 1997)

DVDS
Ancient Egypt: Land Of The Pharaohs/The Pharaohs: Kings Of The Desert (Sanctuary Digital Entertainment, 2001)
Lost Treasures Of The Ancient World – Ancient Egypt (Cromwell Productions, 2003)
Mummies and the Wonders of Ancient Egypt (A & E Entertainment, 2001)

VIDEO
Ancient Egypt (Castle Home Video, 1999)

Index